Pastoral Pointers

Library of Congress Catalog Card Number: 75-18284

ISBN 0-87148-686-5

FOREWORD

For a period of about a year, a very popular feature of the *Church of God Evangel* was a section captioned, *Pastoral Pointers*. As the title implies, this material was written to aid pastors, especially young ministers entering the pastoral field.

The writers of *Pastoral Pointers* are capable, experienced and very successful ministers. Each was selected to write on an assigned subject dealing with an area of the ministry in which he is well versed.

Thinking that the material offered in *Pastoral Pointers* in the various issues of the *Church of God Evangel* could be utilized to an even greater advantage if it were put in book form, the Editorial and Publications Board of the Church of God authorized the printing of this book.

As each reader will soon discover, the content is rich. This book offers practical and easily understood guidance for the pastor who seeks to improve himself and his work as a pastor.

I am of the opinion that all pastors who read this book will treasure it and keep it for a ready reference. Older pastors will appreciate it and will no doubt recommend it to the young minister who perhaps has just accepted his first pastorate.

I wish to acknowledge, with deep gratitude, the writer of each chapter. All of these ministers are very busy ministers, and their willingness to take time from heavy schedules to prepare this material reflects their love and concern for the work of the Lord and for the welfare of their fellow ministers.

We are confident that each pastor who reads this book will be very grateful that he did.

O. W. Polen, D.D.
Editor in Chief
Church of God Publications

Contents

Photo by George Keppler

1

The Pastor's Prayers

By C. E. FRENCH

☐ I would like very much to present a short treatise on this vital subject of prayer in a somewhat different way than is usually pursued. In doing so, let us draw aside from examples and illustrations and human experiences, and listen to the Great Teacher on the matter.

Through close study and scrutiny of the history of Christ's life and practice, one readily sees that He didn't come behind in what He advocated for His fellow ministers whom He ordained as undershepherds. His whole life's image is studded like a precious jewel with bright and glowing experiences of prayer and consecration to His Father. From the desert's forty days of prayer and fasting experience to the final committal in Gethsemane, He pursued a life of public and private prayers. And He laid out a life's prayer plan for each of His followers, as a draftsman might do for a construction project, and bade us observe it meticulously, lest we become hypocritical in our Christian life and practice.

The time element doesn't come out in this simple little message our Saviour is giving. He simply says: "When thou prayest. . . ." With all the other places of prayer mentioned in the Word—such as their homes, the seaside, the Temple and the synagogues, the jail, and other public places—surely no one would contend that Christ intended for men to run away and hide every time they decide to pray. And yet there is no other recorded teaching from the Master on the matter of praying that conveys such forceful and unmistakable words. "When thou prayest, enter into thy closet, and when thou hast shut thy door, pray to thy Father" (Matthew 6:6). To me the tenor of these words and the aspect of command stand out like the sun by day and the moon by night; and, like a clanging sound, they call me often to meet my Father in prayer and secret devotion.

This law of prayer, as set forth by our own lovely Lord Jesus, can be thus summarized: Christ's model for all prayers is summed up in Matthew 6:9-15 and Luke 11:2-4. He is Father; we are sons. Right praying is an act of worship, adoration, and admiration; and it draws from us complete submission and surrender. The true worshiper accepts beforehand, always, the blessed Father's will for his life. So now, with this clarion call coming from the Lord Jesus Christ through the Scriptures, let us go into the closet, close the door, and explore the wonderment of this specific manner of praying.

It is very, very secluded in here. It is quiet in here. Here one becomes aware of Another's presence, and strangely enough, it is easier to accuse oneself than the other Christian. Like Isaiah, one tends to pronounce his own woes rather than the other person's shortcomings. And, strange though it is, we feel freer to discuss ourselves for just what we are and to confess a willingness to adjust our lives as He may direct. We talk (and right here, please allow me to remind you that prayer is a talk with God) about our own sins, if there be any, and our selfish attitudes and ill-conceived ideas and motives. We become freshly aware of relationships with the church, with the family and with all other aspects of life and living. The ear (heart) develops

11

a keenness to the divine voice, and He may call for a confession or acknowledgment of our weakness and total dependence upon Him. He may relate his Garden experience, or He may show you His crowned brow and offer to take you again up Calvary's rugged path. He may ask you to compare your American way of life with that which He endured for your sake and for others. And, my brother pastor, if you stay there long enough, you will hear groanings coming from your innermost being that you have never heard before.

His Spirit will direct your petition. He will put restraints on all your own ways and teach you to walk humbly with Him. Further, as one who knows well, I assure you that He will satiate all your hunger and desires for more of Him.

Will you please read these powerful words in Matthew 6:9-15 a couple of times more and pause and think long on what Christ really meant in verses 5 and 6? Think long on the thought of self and showmanship, and then read them another couple of times. Is there any danger of becoming hypocritical in our praying? Just how careful are we when we know that we are being seen and heard in prayer? What was Christ's purpose when He drew attention to a heathen man's prayer of "much speaking"? Or the Pharisee's "long prayers"?

When a man refuses to closet himself in secret communion with God, his praying ceases to be a force and becomes a farce.

I have tried and proved the faithfulness of our Lord Jesus Christ. I have endured poverty but also have basked in plenty. I have suffered in sickness and have also enjoyed good health. I have rejoiced with soul victory and have persisted under the pressures of cold spiritual desperation. Devils and demons have surrounded me, but God pushed them back with encampments of angels. And I wish to say particularly to the young ministers that Christ will honor them that honor Him and will always bless their faithfulness and obedience.

Now for the expression of one of my deepest and most sincere convictions which I beg you to earnestly consider: no pastor—whether he be an elderly, well-experienced minister or a younger man, who is experiencing all the processes of learning—can live an effective and exemplary Christian life who does not go regularly for this "closed-door" secret prayer.

Photo by H. Armstrong Roberts

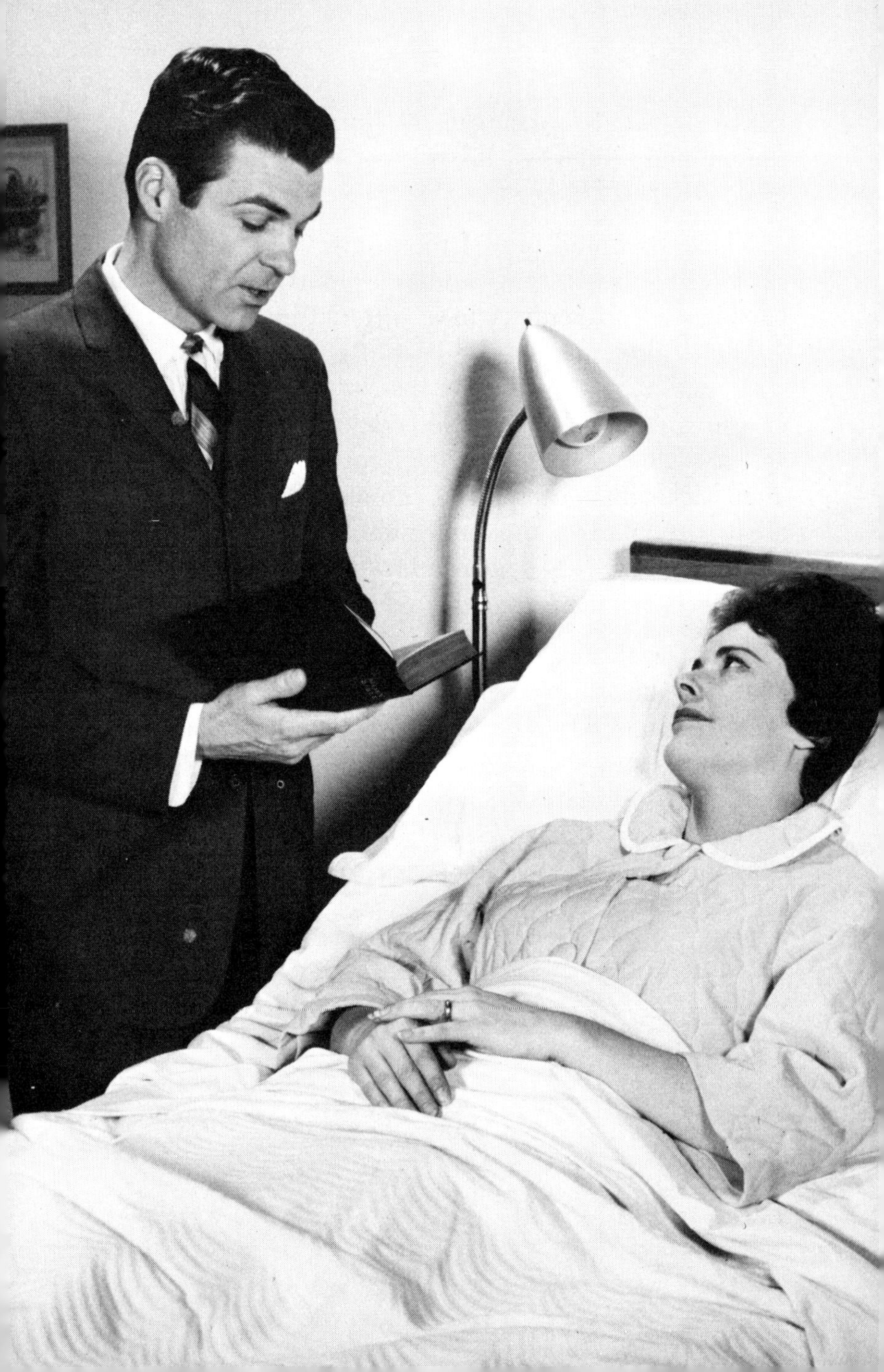

2

The Pastor and Hospital Visitation

By JACK H. ADAMS

I was sick, and ye visited me (Matthew 25:36).

☐ In the Bible we find examples of men visiting their fellowmen in times of sickness: In 2 Kings 13, King Joash visited Elisha, the prophet; Eliphaz, Bildad, Zophar, and Elihu visited Job; and in the twenty-fifth chapter of Matthew, the Lord commends the righteous for the visitation of the sick.

Hospital visitation is a vital part of my ministry. Many good members in my parish were won to

Christ and the church by hospital visitation. I have Sunday school scholars who began coming after hospital visitation.

This is a busy world we live in, and we are trying to reach its people with the gospel. Many times when we try to talk to people in their homes, they have other things they want to do or a television program they wish to watch. They are too busy to talk about the Lord and the church. But, in the hospital it's a different story. When men and women begin to feel pain in the body, and sickness comes upon them, they begin to have a different outlook on life; and they think more soberly. This is a good time to talk with them and to pray with them.

Hospital visitation gives the pastor an opportunity to become better acquainted with his people. He can show his interest in and love for the congregation at a time when people want interest shown.

Even though I have had full-time associate ministers for several years, I take care of most all hospital calls myself. It is my conviction that when people are sick, they want the pastor.

The hospital calls should be made to all the flock, not just the adults. When a member's child or one of the bus children is in the hospital, the pastor should visit him. When one of the congregation turns in the name of a friend or relative who has been hospitalized, this is an open door to reach that individual too.

There are some things a pastor should keep in mind in hospital visitation: (1) The patient is sick and will tire easily. Therefore, he should make his visit short and cheerful. In most cases the visit should not be more than ten minutes in duration. (2) He should not sit on the bed or talk too loudly. (3) He should not talk to a patient about another person's illness or compare the patient's illness to someone else's. (4) He should try not to frighten the patient. (5) He should be cooperative with the hospital staff. (6) He should pray at the close of the visit; most people desire prayer. In praying, he should consider the other patients and not pray so loudly that it will disturb them.

Hospital visitation is a great opportunity for the pastor to show concern and to make friends. It is a time to let the community know he cares. The flock of God needs more loving shepherds who will be about the Father's business in this respect.

James 5:15 says, "The prayer of faith shall save the sick, and the Lord shall raise him up." If we will visit, pray, and have faith, God will heal the sick and restore them to our churches.

Photo by George Keppler

3

The Pastor
and
His Fellow Minister

By T. L. FORESTER

☐ The Apostle Paul was a pastor's pastor, an overseer's overseer, and a preacher's preacher. In Acts
20:28 he said, "Take heed therefore unto yourselves, and to all the flock, over the which the
Holy Ghost hath made you overseers." In this verse
the apostle established the rights, responsibilities,
and importance of a pastor.

The true pastor is an overseer. Although the
word *overseer* is used five times in the Old Testament, it is used only this once in the New Testament. It means that a man is "in general charge
of the church," that he is a "bishop or pastor."

The most honorable, responsible, and exciting position a minister can fill today is the office of a pastor. He cares for, leads, feeds, and watches his flock grow spiritually. There are large and small churches, but there are not large and small pastors. The responsibilities of a pastor in a small church are just as important as those of a pastor in a large church. I have never been privileged to pastor the largest church in any state where I worked, but I have always felt that the church I pastored was the best church in my state.

I think we should take down the code of ethics for Church of God ministers and read it over again. It is a code of ethics that we must live by if we are going to be effective and influential in building this church and carrying out the work which Christ has commissioned us to do. A pastor lives in a glass house. His life is an open book before the public. The public expects more of him. Remember, however, that the true pastor is called of God, ordained of God, and set aside.

It is essential that our relationship with one another be on a very high level. "Be ye kind one to another, tenderhearted, forgiving one another" (Ephesians 4:32). In dealing with our fellow minister, we must always try to place ourselves in his position and circumstances and deal with him as we would like for him to deal with us in the same circumstances. We must be fair with our fellow minister, especially where there is more than one church in a city.

I once received a call from a family who had just moved into town. The lady wanted to keep her two daughters in church and asked for instructions on how to take the bus to the church which I pastored.

When she told me where she lived, I explained that she would have to ride the bus downtown, transfer, and then ride three or four more miles to the church.

"However," I advised, "you pass within two hundred feet of another Church of God before you get downtown. If you would like to stop there, it won't be necessary to transfer; and you will cut down your traveling time. The pastor is a very fine man."

She took my advice, became a member of the other congregation, and reared a family there.

When a pastor is appointed to a new congregation, it is very important for him to cut off contact and remain away from the previous pastorate and city as much as possible. This is very important for the new pastor taking over. The new pastor coming in should be considerate and never criticize the administration of the previous man. It is very easy for us to see the mistakes of others and forget about our own.

A growing concern of mine is the practice of publicizing from the pulpits of our churches—as well as the pulpits of our camp meetings—the errors of fallen ministers. It seems to me that if one wants to talk about the ministry, there are 99 percent of our ministers whose lives have never been touched or tainted by sin. They have lived holy, conducted themselves in an upright manner, and lived sacrificially to preach this blessed gospel. Talk about them and the whole ministry of this church will be looked upon with higher esteem.

The true pastor's motivation springs from the example of Jesus Christ, who Himself is the Chief Shepherd (1 Peter 5:4).

4

The Pastor and the Funeral

By W. T. AINSWORTH

☐ The words *pastor* and *shepherd* are the same, in that they both pertain to a ministry of caring for the needs of the flock. "And he gave some, apostles; and some, prophets; and some, evangelists; and some, pastors and teachers" (Ephesians 4:11).

Pastors or shepherds are God-given men with hearts of understanding and love for the needs of God's people. The pastor has love, in that he has been ordained of God to manifest the Word of God in action toward those that belong to Christ. He has understanding in that he has been enlightened in the mysteries of life and death and in the reality of eternity.

The pastor is also God's ambassador to convey the will of a loving God to those that are in need. One of the most important aspects of a pastor's calling is ministering to those who have lost a loved one in death.

The telephone rings, and there is a concerned voice, speaking, "Pastor, our loved one is not expected to live through the night. Would you please come to the hospital quickly?"

As a pastor, you reach for your coat. As you proceed to the hospital, you pray: "Lord, help me to be a blessing to the dying and to the bereaved."

As you enter the hospital room, the family is standing quietly waiting in hope as they look to you for comfort. Your concern is for the sick one, but as he succumbs to death, you turn your attention to the family. You avoid showing signs of grief in order to help the family and their friends.

Amid the different reactions to death, you endeavor to be understanding. Some will blame themselves; others will become withdrawn and silent; others will endeavor to withhold any show of emotion. The presence of a pastor will help to relieve the shock of losing a loved one.

When the doctor and nurse are finished with

the family, you invite them to a quiet place. There you can minister to their various needs.

Many thoughts flood your mind: *Was the patient a Christian? How can I be of help to the family?* You know that there are no words that will give full satisfaction for the broken heart. Only the Word of God can comfort in such an hour.

Avoid giving cheap consolation. Realize that as the pastor you represent to the bereaved the values of religious faith such as forgiveness, immortality, hope, and the goodness of God toward every individual.

Such statements as, "He would not have you to grieve this way" or, "You have lost but he has gained" should be avoided. Say, instead, "I cannot express adequately my sorrow at this time." Then try to help the bereaved one to accept the pain of bereavement.

In planning the funeral service, acquaint yourself with the background of the deceased one and his family. This will be helpful in planning the service.

Contact those that are to be involved as to the time and place of the service. If the family states a preference to do so, welcome another minister to assist in the services.

After the program for the service has been arranged, contact the funeral director and give him the necessary information. He, in turn, will give you, the pastor, the obituary notice that you will read in the service.

Having visited the family in their home before the service, you then proceed to the chapel. The goal of the service is to extend comfort and hope to the bereaved. Therefore, endeavor to avoid using words or songs that would open the wound.

As a pastor, you realize how much the family members are depending on you; and you are depending on the Holy Spirit and the Word to bring hope to the family and friends.

When you step to the podium, you know that you have an opportunity to speak to people that may never have heard, or may never hear again, a message from God's Holy Word. So you interweave golden threads of hope into the message, to the sinner as well as to the child of God.

An inspirational conclusion to the message is 1 Thessalonians 4:15-18.

> *For this we say unto you by the word of the Lord, that we which are alive and remain unto the coming of the Lord shall not prevent them which are asleep. For*

*the Lord h i m s e l f shall descend from
heaven with a shout, with the voice of
the archangel, and with the trump of
God: and the dead in Christ shall rise
first: Then we which are alive and remain shall be caught up together with
them in the clouds, to meet the Lord in
the air: and so shall we ever be with the
Lord. Wherefore comfort one another
with these words.*

The minister will find that he can have a most
effective ministry with a bereaved family. They
will appreciate his kindness, and he will have an
opportunity to share with them eternal truths. It is
the living, not the dead, who make the funeral
service significant.

5

Pastoral Counseling

By DR. PAUL L. WALKER

☐ In Margaret Mitchell's novel *Gone With the Wind*, Will Benteen delivers an oration at Mr. O'Hara's funeral which states the case of many people in our churches and communities. Will says, "Everybody's mainspring is different. And I want to say this—folks whose mainsprings are busted are better dead." Because of strained and broken mental and spiritual mainsprings, the pastor of our day is called upon to adapt his pastoral ministry to dealing with specific persons who approach him for help with specific problems. This necessitates pastoral counseling and suggests that the pastor give close attention to a three-dimensional model of the counseling pastor.

DIMENSION 1: Pastoral
Counseling Is Derived
From Pastoral Care.

The pastoral role is not an easy one. It involves multiple activities, but the successful pastor is the one who is able to integrate these into a unified function as the shepherd-leader who sincerely cares about the spiritual and personal growth of his parish. In this role the pastor seeks to lead persons toward the achievement of positive adjustment to God, to themselves, and to other persons. Thus, within this broad context we can define *pastoral care* as "the pastor's oversight of the personal and family needs of his people."

One facet of the pastoral ministry generated by effective pastoral care is the ministry of counseling. Pastoral counseling may be defined as a way of facing problems together with a needy person toward the goal of gaining new understanding and developing new responsibility whereby constructive solutions can be worked out by appropriate action. When effective pastoral care is administered, pastoral counseling should be initiated in the following areas:

1. Pastoral counseling should offer an opportunity for complete and open confession to God by

the person without fear of the counselor's blame, hostility, or betrayal of confidence.

2. Pastoral counseling should offer a deepening meditative introspection by the person to bring the unconscious into the conscious and the positive exertion of the will to master the emotions.

3. Pastoral counseling should offer a means of lifting the person's self-esteem so that he sees himself as a person of intrinsic value and worth to be treasured rather than a thing to be manipulated or degraded.

4. Pastoral counseling should involve a dependence upon the Holy Spirit in which the counselor is freed from the temptation to play God and the person is enabled to grow in grace as he accepts the counselor as a fellow human being interested in his welfare.

DIMENSION 2: Pastoral
Counseling Is a Personal
Way of Life.

Counseling is not done by an object or a blank screen. Pastoral counseling demands the modeling behavior and Christian maturity of an effective Christian pastor. The pastor brings himself (both strengths and weaknesses) into every counseling session. In essence the pastor must develop a facilitative personality characterized by spiritual maturity if he is to counsel efficiently.

Becoming a facilitator means the following:

1. The pastor lives effectively himself. *Prayer* *Dedication*

2. The pastor relates to people in a constructive and genuine manner. *Same Troubles* *similar circumstances*

3. The pastor strives to achieve an accurate, empathic understanding of people's feelings and private worlds. *enter into their feelings (anxieties)*

4. The pastor responds to people at both a feeling and experiential level. *cry with those, joy*

5. The pastor learns to create a climate of acceptance and positive regard for people regardless of the circumstance or situation. *come unto Christ all*

6. The pastor learns how to be assertive and confrontive in an appropriate and nurturing attitude. *Positive statements of Scripture considerate for their Troubles*

7. The pastor develops a response style that labels feelings, facilitates action, and maintains respect and confidence. *Gaining - discreet attitudes*

8. The pastor strives to model the Christ ideal as a shepherd-leader who truly cares and wants to help. *Point to the Savior always as the Remedy for all ills encourage faith and trust look for Lack of Love bitterness, selfishness Etc.*

34

DIMENSION 3: Pastoral
Counseling Emphasizes the
Variables of Therapeutic
Change Within a Scriptural
Framework.

Research has shown that the degree to which certain relationship variables are present determines the degree to which therapeutic change and help occurs. These variables include empathy, congruence, respect, concreteness, and confrontation. When these are placed in a scriptural framework and utilized in the relationship between a pastor and a troubled person, the stage is set for spiritual enrichment and genuine behavior change.

Empathy, based on Ephesians 4:31, 32 and 1 Corinthians 13, means "entering the person's private world and communicating that one understands, cares, and is willing to help." *Empathy* is "intense sensitivity to another person's feelings and experiences."

Congruence is based on 2 Corinthians 3:18 and suggests that the pastor be himself in "an honest and forthright manner." It means being what one really is at the particular moment in "an open and flexible attitude devoid of bias and exploitative motives."

Respect, based on 1 John 1:7-10 and 2:1, 2, calls for the pastor to "prize" the person as being of extreme value and worth regardless of the situation.

Concreteness is based on Ephesians 4:29 and involves the importance of "fluent, direct, and simple speech patterns." It connotes "clarity, interpretation, and opportunities for honest feedback."

Confrontation, based on 1 John 2:3-6, offers the opportunity for "assertive and direct behavior that promotes constructive action and effective resolution."

In summary, pastoral counseling is one facet of the pastoral ministry that is generated by effective pastoral care. Counseling is a necessity in this *age of anxiety* and *broken mainsprings* if the church is truly to minister to persons and individual needs. Thus, to be effective, the pastor must learn to function in a three-dimensional model of shepherd-leader, facilitator, and agent for therapeutic change.

Photo by George Keppler

6

The Pastor and His Dress

By BOB LYONS

☐ Pastoring as a profession presents a multifarious set of problems r e l a t i n g to dress. The minister must function as pastor, priest, and prophet. In addition, he is a human being with needs, emotions, and desires. His clothing, while being basic to his role, exemplifies a diversity of expression. It has been stated that clothes make the man. Obviously, this statement is not entirely correct. Clothes, in and of themselves, simply fill a functional need relating to the very special profession in life called the ministry.

The question of pastoral dress connotes a very unique set of problems. First, no two people will ever agree on the mode of dress. Something will always be too loud, too eccentric, or too sedate! Second, the dress question has never, to my knowledge, been directed toward the ministry; but it is always the minister telling others, specifically the ladies, how they should or should not dress. Therefore, I do not pretend to be a connoisseur of correct dress nor even insinuate that what I have to offer by way of suggestion is either universally accepted or uniquely mine.

In approaching the subject of the pastor and his dress, I notice that several facts are glaringly obvious. First, the minister must realize that the nature of his work places him constantly in the limelight. Everybody in the congregation knows when the preacher acquires a new suit, shirt, or even a new tie. If the suit is contemporary or well-designed and tailored, at least one member will remark, "I wish I were a preacher so I could wear clothes like that." On the other hand, if a minister went to the factory and bought one at a "ministerial discount," and if it wasn't the very best, but was all he could afford on his meager income, some individual would be determined to announce to all who would listen, "Our preacher sure does dress sloppy." The same old game—not being able to win for losing!

The above point does raise the vital principle that the dress of a minister should be appropriate to those he serves. The rural pastor could wear a less formal dress in his pastoral work than a metropolitan minister. Is it necessarily right or wrong? No; it is the simple measure of acclimating to a specific cultural environment.

Second, the minister must recognize that sociological studies have proven that the clergyman along with doctors are high-risk targets for sexual overtures. Mysticism of the ministry, the vicious hatred by Satan for the "man of the cloth," and the hero image all contribute to this delicate dilemma. Ministers can dress just as provocatively as the ladies of the church. The current trend in men's fashion is toward femininity rather than masculinity. Males have become just as conscious of fashions of hair and dress as females. The minister is susceptible to the innuendos of cultural and social change.

The minister should dress appropriately and avoid extremes because of his solemn function in handling holy and serious matters. Pastors, while avoiding gaudy shirts and flamboyant ties on one extreme and the black, austere, never-smile, stick-in-the-mud stereotype on the other hand, cannot afford an image of showmanship.

The arena of the ministerial occupation has by its very nature certain built-in crises as they relate to the minister's dress. Ministers who come from rural backgrounds do not lean toward formal dress such as robes or clerical collars. The normal reaction is to classify those wearing clerical collars as formal; and if formal, therefore, less spiritual; and if less spiritual, then worldly. The logic of this rationale is preposterous. What a minister wears does not necessarily determine his spirituality, but may only speak of his preference, based upon cultural background.

In summation, may I suggest that neither these few remarks nor a voluminous work equal to the *Encyclopaedia Britannica* will ever be accepted as a final definitive word on the topic of pastoral dress. There are a few insights which have commonality in the Church of God, and it would be beneficial for us to reflect upon them: One, remember that wherever, whenever, and whatever you are doing, the preacher is the representative of God and minister to those he serves. Two, neatness and appropriateness are not insured by the purchase of a $250 suit, nor is it eliminated by a suit which costs only $25. Three, always ask yourself, Does my mode of dress violate any biblical principle of moderation or does it isolate me from the people? Four, consider, Am I being honest with myself, with God, and with those I serve when I wear this particular article of clothing?

7

The Pastor and the Church Council

By FLOYD L. McCLUNG

☐ The pastor's relationship to the church council is found in the larger principles of the responsibilities for church government set down in Scripture. These principles include the pastor's duty to serve, his duty to lead, and the duty of the council and congregation to follow the spiritual leadership of the pastor.

The pastor serves as overseer and not the overlord in the local church, and he must ever keep in mind that he is by no means the first in command. There is definite scriptural authority given to the pastor, but he dare not assume that it gives him the right to carnal rulership.

The pastor himself is under the orders of Jesus Christ; and, as undershepherd of the flock, he is dealt with in tender love by the hand of the divine administrator. With this biblical concept firmly established in the mind of the pastor, he will endeavor to lead the local flock of God in a spirit of love and genuine humility.

Webster says that an *administrator* is "one who manages, governs, or directs affairs, or is capable of doing so." The pastor is placed as leader of the local church to manage and direct the affairs of the church.

But woe be to the pastor who does not first get his orders from heaven, and woe be to the pastor who feels that because he is in a position of leadership that he has the right to assume that he is an authority on every subject and that he knows more about everything around the church than anyone else!

This does not mean that the pastor is to do all the work around the church and be merely a "glorified errand boy" for those who feel that they have been especially commissioned to tell the pastor how, when, and where he is to do his work. But it is a wise man who is willing to spread responsibility and allow men to function within the framework of the church. D. L. Moody said, "It is better to put ten men to work than it is to do the work of ten men."

It is a rare thing for a pastor's scriptural authority to be questioned if he is functioning as a true spiritual administrator. If the pastor loves his people and lets them know it, most of them will stand shoulder to shoulder in the work with him.

The remarks often made about church council members being hard to get along with are deplorable. Some preachers are hard to get along with, too. It is said that the sheep take on the characteristics of their shepherd. If he is calm, quiet, peaceful, patient, and trusting, the sheep will adopt the same manner; but if he is loud, nervous, demanding, forceful, restless, and fearful, then he will have that kind of sheep. Pastors have a great responsibility to their people to be in themselves what they expect the people to be.

In the pastor-and-church-council relationship the pastor does not lower his dignity, or jeopardize his position by allowing thinking men to disagree with him on some things. The strongest leadership is not that of a hard dictatorial spirit, but that of a dedicated, tender, and sacrificial spirit. A man is not worth his salt who does not have firm convictions and is willing to stand for right and principle when necessary, but he cannot be a successful pastor if he cannot love and respect those who disagree with him.

A wise pastor will allow his council to function according to the guidelines established by the General Assembly. Areas of responsibility will be assigned, and trust and confidence will be placed in these men as co-laborers in the work of the Lord. Remember: some of these men are perhaps better qualified to do some things than the pastor is, although this is the acid test of humility for him to be willing to admit it.

A wise pastor will understand that mistakes will be made, and he will be kind enough not to be always bringing them up as reminders. A wise pastor will not insist that his plan be carried out exactly as he thinks. If it is a God-given plan, he will carry it in his heart; and if there are reverses and delays, he will always be gracious and cheerful.

Time has a way of getting lots of things done that would prove divisive if done right now. It is sometimes best, then, to lay aside something that might bring division until it is possible to do it without controversy. Here the grace of patience must prevail if unity is to be maintained.

Now let us examine the pastor's position as

leader of the flock, and this includes the church council. By virtue of his office the pastor is in command, and this is the Bible plan. The Bible knows of no other plan.

All down the centuries it has been the same. When God wanted something done, He chose a man, equipped, and fitted him for the task, placed him at the head of His people, and told them to follow and obey.

This places the pastor in a place of awesome responsibility. He is to lead the people of God, not drive them. The words of Jacob illustrate this point very clearly: "My lord knoweth that the children are tender, and the flocks and herds with young are with me: and if men should overdrive them one day, all the flock will die. Let my lord, I pray thee, pass over before his servant: *and I will lead on softly*" (Genesis 33:13, 14).

It requires both genius and grace to "lead on softly," but it can be done. God will furnish the grace and the wise pastor will acquire the genius.

To deal softly does not mean one is compromising his sacred position of leadership. It might gain respect from those who bring opposition if they would see this demonstration of tender loving care for the flock of God.

A pastor needs to "lead on softly" in the pulpit, and "lead on softly" in the relationships to those with whom he must work closely within the church. Remember: church councils are formed, not to control and command, not to dictate, but to cooperate and assist their God-chosen leader. With mutual love and respect between pastor and church council a team can be formed to lead a congregation in spiritual growth, numerical increase, and financial blessings.

The truth of Ephesians 4:11, 12 can be demonstrated in this setting: "And he gave some, apostles; and some, prophets; and some, evangelists; and some, pastors and teachers; For the perfecting of the saints, for the work of the ministry, for the edifying of the body of Christ."

The essence of the passage seems to say that it is the responsibility of those who are called to fill the offices as listed in verse 11 to train and equip the saints that they might do the work of ministry. What greater privilege could a pastor have than to share his burden with his council for the work of ministry until they would catch this burden and vision? The whole congregation soon senses this combined ministry effort, which produces a unity of spirit that is evident to all.

As the leader follows Christ, you will follow him; for God's plan is that His flock be led by a shepherd, not run by a board or committee. Church councils are to advise and assist, never to dictate. The Holy Spirit anoints men.

8

Pulpit Ethics

By HOMER G. RHEA, JR.

☐ The sacred role of the pastor in the pulpit is discussed by J. H. Jowett in his book *The Preacher: His Life and Work.* He writes: "The pulpit may be the center of overwhelming power, and it may be the scene of tragic disaster. . . . It is our God-appointed office to lead men and women who are weary or wayward, exultant or depressed, eager or indifferent, into 'the secret place of the Most High.' We are to help the sinful to the fountain of cleansing, the bondslaves to the wonderful songs of deliverance. . . . We are to help the broken-winged into the healing light of 'the heavenly places in Christ Jesus.' We are to help the sad into the sunshine of grace. . . . This is something of what our calling means when we enter the pulpit of the sanctuary. And our possible glory is this, we may do it. And our possible shame is this, we may hinder it." Realizing these worthy objectives require *earnestness, courtesy,* and *preparation.*

Earnestness

The pastor's conduct in the pulpit should reflect who he is and whose he is. If he is God's servant, his heart will radiate warmth. If the pastor is commissioned by the dying Savior to declare His love and reap the reward of His wounds, he will minister earnestly. If the Lord has anointed him to preach, he will rely upon His strength. If he is divinely called, his ministry will take on an eternal dimension. The pastor belongs to a nobler order and to a higher fraternity than that which is found on this earth. Thus, he should gauge his ministry by the light of the Judgment Day and in view of the eternal rewards of faithfulness. He knows that the joy of seeing a soul saved is overwhelmingly delightful. How wonderful it will be at the Day of Judgment for him to meet spirits redeemed by Christ—spirits who learned the news of their redemption from his lips!

Courtesy

The pastor's pulpit manners should include those common civilities that become a gentleman, especially a Christian gentleman. Such courtesy will restrain the pastor from making derogatory remarks about fellow ministers, his own denomination, or other denominations. Discretion will be used in making personal references while delivering the sermon. Careful acknowledgement and due respect will be shown as he addresses the congregation.

A pastor's attitude toward a guest minister is important. The minister is his guest and should be treated with all the thoughtfulness and consideration that one would give to a guest. Needless talking and whispering should be avoided. The pulpit is not the place for social conversation. This can only serve to distract the people from the spirit of worship. The pastor's pulpit manners reflect his qualifications to be a representative of the church and the pastor of a body of people.

Preparation

A pastor is a preacher of the gospel before he is anything else. His main business is to study and to know the Scriptures and to impart this knowledge to the constituents. The surgeon's task, which results in healing, is to repair malfunctioning parts of the body. In this he needs great skill. If he should be able to belt an angel with a girdle of gold and cannot successfully perform an operation, he will fail as a surgeon.

Whatever else a minister may excel in, he has not done his greatest work until he has brought the people to God and God to the people through the Word. How important it is that you meditate day and night in the law of the Lord! A heart fully prepared through prayer, study, and divine anointing will bear a message from God which will edify the church.

Photo by George Keppler

9

The Pastor and His Sermon Preparation

By J. FRANK SPIVEY

☐ One of the most important items on the pastor's weekly schedule of activities is the preparation of sermons he is to deliver. To many ministers this presents a real dilemma—to others it seems to create no problem at all. To some it is sheer drudgery—to others a delight.

Could the difficulties incurred in this area of a man's ministry be in the fact that he undertakes this task without sufficient self-preparation? I am afraid that the answer is yes.

Far too many pastors think of their sermons in terms of last-minute preparation. Late in the week they tear themselves away from the dozen less-important things that have been allowed to claim their attention all week long. They run into their study, sit down at their desk or typewriter, and attempt to place on paper, in logical form, a few thoughts—all the while hoping that the result on Sunday morning will be something that might be called a sermon.

To me, there are at least two aspects of sermon preparation. The first I call, "The Preparation *for* the Sermon"; the second, "The Preparation *of* the the Sermon." One has to do with the man—the other with the message. Both are vitally important. If either is left out, the sermon will suffer as a result.

Let us think briefly about the preparation of the man. I am not speaking here of colleges attended, of degrees acquired, or of any other scholastic attainment—although I readily acknowledge their value—but I refer to that spiritual preparation which is so necessary to every man's ministry.

I am quite sure this is partially what the Apostle Paul had in mind when he met with the ministers at the church in Ephesus and left this solemn command: "Take heed therefore unto yourselves, and to all the flock, over the which the Holy Ghost hath made you overseers, to feed the church of

God, which he hath purchased with his own blood" (Acts 20:28).

Paul makes one thing unmistakably clear—his first concern was not with the message, but the messenger. "Take heed . . . unto yourselves." The pastor who is careless about his own spirituality will have little or no concern about the spiritual need of his church.

Complying with Paul's requirement will demand personal sacrifice and discipline. It will mean giving the proper amount of time, consistently and systematically, to seeking the Lord with prayer and fasting for our own personal spiritual enrichment. It will not be easy, but it will be rewarding.

Perhaps J. H. Jowett expressed it best when he said:

> We must sternly and systematically make time for prayer and the devotional reading of the Word of God. We must appoint private seasons for deliberate and personal appropriation of the divine Word; for self-examination in the presence of its warnings; for self-humbling in the presence of its judgments; for self-heartening in the presence of its promises; and, for self-invigoration in the presence of its hopes.

The minister who neglects this type of communion and fellowship does so at his own peril. But the minister who will accept the challenge will find the living water so refreshing, the power and presence of the Holy Spirit so revitalizing, and the living Word so enriching that his problem of planning and preparation of sermons will become a joy instead of a chore.

The old Negro preacher in the Deep South was not too far afield when he was asked how he came to preach such masterful sermons. He replied, "I reads myself full; I prays myself hot; and, I lets myself go."

It has long been my contention that every preacher ought to preach out of the overflow of his own experience. This can happen only when we have lingered long in His holy presence. It is also my conviction that sermons are not made— they grow, and they can only grow and develop successfully in the rich and fertile soil of a deep devotional life.

The pastor that will bring this kind of self-preparation to bear on his sermon planning will have no trouble finding and developing a text, for texts will be there in plentiful supply.

The text, finally chosen, will be one that you

have seen often in all its radiant beauty, in your private excursions into the secret place of the Most High. The path you follow in its development will be one that you have walked in your hours of communion and fellowship with Him. The truth you present will come from the living Word that has been eaten and digested in the deep recesses of your own soul, so that you will be able to preach not only out of the Word but out of your experience also. Upon the deliverance of the sermon, the church will be able to say of you as Paul said of Onesiphorus, "He oft refreshed me" (2 Timothy 1:16).

10

The Pastor
and
His Library

By J. E. DeVORE

☐ In 1 Timothy 4:6, 13 Paul spoke of "A good minister of Jesus Christ, nourished up in the words of faith and of good doctrine . . . Till I come, give attendance to reading, to exhortation, to doctrine."

Paul loved his books, especially the Holy Scriptures. What a pastor he must have been! What a preacher he must have been!

It has been said that you are what you read. You are the product of your reading. One busy pastor complained, "If this is true, I am nothing, I am zero, because I have no time to give attendance to reading."

The Reverend George Alford, beloved Bible teacher, has said, "I have only one regret. I regret that I have not spent more time in that blessed old Book [the Holy Bible]." No matter how busy, how occupied we become in the ministry, we must take time to read and pray every day. If we do not feed our own souls, we will eventually run out of food for others.

You and I are living in a fast-paced world. As ministers we are charged to communicate the gospel message to men. To fulfill our obligation to feed them with spiritual food, we must be aware of their problems and must constantly seek for those answers that will make the gospel more meaningful to them. Blessed is the minister who can find those answers upon his knees in prayer and in his library!

We look for flowers in a garden. We look for fruit in an orchard. We look for trees in a forest. We look for beauty in the sunset. We look for honey in a beehive. We listen for laughter on a playground. We look for Holy Ghost manifestations in a Pentecostal service. We look for words in a dictionary and for books in a library. We especially look for books that will bless the pastor to bless his people in his library. We must be inspired ourselves before we can inspire others.

This exigent life (requiring much of us and requiring it immediately) requires that we have our tools sharp, our equipment organized, ready always for immediate use. In anticipation of the work before us as pastors, we should prepare accordingly. Those who are called to the ministry, for example, who have the privilege of attending Bible college and seminary, should keep their textbooks and notes.

If I could go back twenty-eight years to the beginning of my ministry, I would start with a good study Bible such as *Thompson Chain-Reference,* a *Cruden's Complete Concordance,* and two or three modern translations for comparison with the King James Version. I would build my library according to the list of books recommended for those who plan to be exhorters, then licensed ministers, then ordained. I would buy a manual on wedding ceremonies, funerals, etc., from our Church of God Publishing House.

After building this basic library, I would carefully add books to it from time to time to enhance my preaching and counseling ministry. I would also be interested in books on church administration, Sunday school growth, etc.

I would keep notes and a simple record system

on all my reading and study. As I continued to build my library, I would concentrate on Church of God and Pentecostal authors. I would visit often in my books, but I would live in the Book of books.

A lifetime is not long enough to master all that is contained in that sacred library of sixty-six blessed books. It has been said that in the writings of John in the New Testament there are shallow places where a child could wade and depths where a strong man would have to swim. This is true of every portion and passage through all the precious Word of God. I would buy commentaries on the Bible and read them; but, most of all, I would read the Bible.

The author is anonymous; the source is unknown to me; but I believe it was an aged saint of God who said:

> *We've traveled together, my*
> *Bible and I,*
> *Through all kinds of weath-*
> *er, with smile or with*
> *sigh!*
> *In sorrow or sunshine, in*
> *tempest or calm!*
> *Thy friendship unchanging,*
> *my lamp and my*
> *psalm.*

So now who shall part us,
my Bible and I?
Shall "isms" or schisms, or
"new lights" who try?
Shall shadow for substance,
or stone for good bread,
Supplant thy sound wisdom,
give folly instead?

Ah, no, my dear Bible, ex-
ponent of light!
Thou sword of the Spirit,
put error to flight!
And still through life's
journey, until my last
sigh,
We'll travel together, my Bi-
ble and I.

Adolph Bedsole said, "Young Preacher, learn all you can about everything you can as long as you can." He was saying, "Read books." He was saying, "No knowledge rightly used is wasted. All knowledge can be dedicated to the glory of God if properly used by the preacher." He went on to say, "The preacher who is habitually idle in his study will find himself habitually empty in the pulpit," drawing blanks in the middle of his message.

Yes, Young Pastor, build your library. Read and study your books. And live in your Bible. Then, you will speak with holy authority. You will have a message from God for the people. You will bless them.

11

The Pastor
and
His Family

By O. C. McCANE

☐ The pastor, by virtue of his calling, must lend a Christian influence to the community. He must show by personal example what the life of a Christian is.

The pastor should be possessed with the inescapable conviction that he has been called by God. In Old Testament times, this necessity of a priest, prophet, or judge being divinely selected, was enforced with the fact that a man would experience death if he entered these offices apart from the direct instructions of God.

Paul wrote that he was an apostle—not of men, neither by man, but by Jesus Christ, and God the

73

Father, who raised him from the dead (Galatians 1:1). Paul made this claim again in 1 Timothy 1:12. The advice of Christian leaders and the instruction of the Holy Scripture is that a pastor must feel that he is "a man sent from God."

Although a pastor must keep in mind that he is primarily a servant, he should avoid losing respect as a minister just for the purpose of gaining the approval of a person or class. As pastor, he must never shown favoritism to any individual or side with factions within the church. He is a shepherd —servant to all—and must learn, with God's help, to measure his work not in terms of salary but service.

The Pastor's Role as a Person

As a person the pastor needs to learn what it means to promote the growth of the whole man instead of merely giving lip service to this idea. His life must involve a vital experience of spiritual, mental, and physical development. By a vital and creative experience, we mean one which gives genuine meaning to the total life and work of the pastor and his human relationships. All habits that would be detrimental to a proper influence in any of these spheres of development must be avoided.

Before a pastor can expect to be respected by others, he must first develop a personal confidence. This will be preceded by the acceptance of himself and his responsibility.

Within the role of his personal life he should regard time for prayer and study in the preparation of his messages as sacred. As a minister of the gospel, he is challenged to help people discover, in a meaningful experience, the application of this "good news," to their common-life experiences and crises. He must be "an example of the believers, in word, in conversation, in charity, in spirit, in faith, in purity" (1 Timothy 4:12).

The Pastor's Role in Sharing Christian Values

Another important role of the pastor is the creation and preservation of Christian values. This is really what gives meaning to our church involvement. The participation in these values is what gives significance, ultimately, to our individual Christian life. Only insofar as personal Christian values are fostered can pastors effectively help others change from their way of living, that forever threatens them, to the finer life that follows the example of Christ.

Pastors are individually nothing except in relation to that greater reality—God. Unless we have this personal relationship with God, we and those with whom we worship, will experience dearth in the midst of plenty, squalor in the presence of riches, and spiritual war instead of peace of soul.

The Pastor's Role in Family Responsibilities

A pastor cannot really help other families until he has first challenged his own family to Christian commitment. Paul said that a bishop must be "one that ruleth well his own house, having his children in subjection with all gravity" (1 Timothy 3:4).

The spiritual strength of the pastor's family is vitally important to the spiritual strength of his church. The pastor's example as a father, along with the example of his wife and children is of equal importance to the success of his work for God.

Because of his busy schedule, a pastor is tempted to forget that as a father he is also the spiritual leader of his own family. Yet, the pastor's family is also an institution of God, and he must feel his responsibility to help it fulfill its purpose.

A healthy wholeness in family relationship will mean that the pastor-father will take the lead in recovering the central spiritual role the family plays in teaching by example, godliness, and Christian character.

The influence of the father in the spiritual leadership of the home is unmistakable. Paul wrote, "And, ye fathers, provoke not your children to wrath: but bring them up in the nurture and admonition of the Lord" (Ephesians 6:4).

The three commandments in Deuteronomy 6: 4-7 must be practiced in the pastor's home as well as in all families: (1) "Thou shalt love the Lord thy God"; (2) "These words . . . shall be in thine heart"; and (3) "Thou shalt teach them diligently unto thy children."

Photo by George Keppler

12

The Pastor and Weddings

By THOMAS GRASSANO

☐ One of a pastor's more pleasant duties is uniting a couple in marriage. The true pastor regards the pleasure of this performance as more than just a service. For, to the couple, the wedding is the most important event in their lives.

God instituted marriage. "Therefore shall a man leave his father and his mother, and shall cleave unto his wife: and they shall be one flesh" (Genesis 2:24). God intended that two people become one in interest and above all, one in affection.

From the very beginning of their marriage their thoughts are to be for each other. Their plans are to be mutual. Their joys and sorrows are to be shared alike. And their vows are to be sacred all throughout life.

Marriage is linked with God and the church; therefore the pastor should realize the gravity of the wedding and the privilege of such a service. Pastors should not allow themselves to become "marrying parsons," excusing themselves with the line: "If I don't marry them, someone else will."

As a pastor I have refused to marry certain couples because of problems which existed or because the individuals were incompatible.

Oftentimes persons who have no church connections and who have been married a number of times seek to find a minister to officiate at their wedding. But the minister must be cautious; for, in giving the marriage vows to a husband and wife, he is attesting that they are receiving the blessing of the church.

The place of the wedding usually will determine the procedure of the ceremony. Church weddings are usually the most formal and ceremonial, but this need not be the case. If a couple desires a church wedding, it can be simple and informal, yet sacred.

The church should be the place for the wedding, whether the ceremony is elaborate or informal. The spiritual sacredness of the house of God harmonizes with the significance of marriage itself.

A rehearsal is essential in formal church weddings. Whoever directs the wedding (in many areas this person is the pastor) should arrange a wedding procedure for the parties. This will help to eliminate confusion.

In a wedding the couple is solemnizing their vows before God. I have attended weddings where the ceremony took on a carnivallike performance. Often the photographer was on the platform with his camera lights flashing everywhere during the ceremony. This takes away from the sacredness of the ceremony. There is a proper time and place to take pictures—pictures that will be cherished in years to come.

If the wedding is performed in the church, the home, or the minister's residence, the event should still be special. There is no set style for the ceremony; each pastor should use the form that seems appropriate for that occasion.

Every pastor should familiarize himself with state laws on marriage. Some states require clergymen to register with the city clerk before they are permitted to solemnize marriages.

Before the marriage is performed, the pastor should examine the marriage license to see that it is in legal form.

The pastor's role in premarital counseling is an important part of his ministry. As a shepherd he has a responsibility to couples seeking to be married. The wise pastor will prepare himself. "Counsel in the heart of man is like deep water; but a man of understanding will draw it out" (Proverbs 20:5). Couples will also need shepherding after the solemnizing of their marriage.

The wedding should be a happy feast in which Christ is honored, not only in the service performed but also in the years to come.

Photo by George Keppler

13

The Minister's Voice

By ROOSEVELT MILLER

> *And even things without life giving sound, whether pipe or harp, except they give a distinction in the sounds, how shall it be known what is piped or harped? For if the trumpet give an uncertain sound, who shall prepare himself to the battle?* (1 Corinthians 14:7, 8).

☐ Are you satisfied with your voice? If so, beware. Remember: you may be hearing only the compliments. An absence of criticism may lead to self-satisfaction, and the memory of an early compliment may be a decided handicap.

Have you ever been hurt by comments concerning your voice or speech? Well, don't be offended! Remember: bad habits creep upon a person easily. Hearing one's voice as others hear him would be beneficial, and this is possible with modern recording equipment.

How does your voice sound to you? Don't answer this question *aloud,* but ask yourself how you *think* it sounds. Be honest. Are you satisfied with what you hear?

Does your voice bother you at times while preaching? If so, something you are doing is causing this hindrance. It could be many factors; such as, improper breathing, poor posture habits, improper placement of tones, rigidity, and tension.

Speech is "the art or manner of the oral expression of thought." Thought is the most important factor, but the one who projects the thought well is he who has learned the *art* and *manner.*

THE VOICE

Of all the musical instruments in the world, only the voice has "soul." The voice can praise God as no other instrument can. The voice can feel the depth of sorrow and the height of joy.

The voice enables a person to express what no other instrument can express.

Feelings can be expressed by the voice in a way unequaled by any instrument. The vocal communication of love expresses depth of feeling to the heart of a lover, and no explanation or interpretation is needed. The preached Word from the voice of an anointed minister is carried by the Holy Spirit to the hearers and penetrates the heart, causing them to have faith and to believe on the Lord Jesus Christ. The voice is a wonderful creation—God's gift to man for communicating the greatest message to the world.

POSTURE

Physical freedom is a necessity if one is to be able to speak, preach, or sing at his top potential. The abdominal muscles, the diaphragm, the chest, the neck, the throat, the tongue, and the lips are all used in tone production. A complete coordination and function of these parts is necessary for the free and unrestricted sounds of speech and song.

One voice teacher uses a formula: "Action plus position equals breath." Another says: "Posture plus breathing equals good tones." Naturally, there is much more to producing a good tone than just posture and breath. The point here is to stress that correct physical posture is essential for good diaphragmatic breathing.

Although the first and most essential concern is correct breathing, without good posture, diaphragmatic breathing would be void of the timbre needed for favorable resonant, natural, sonorous tones. Therefore, correct posture gives security and strength to the torso; it allows for complete freedom and coordination of the muscles and provides the greatest possible concentration, intensity, and volume of tone.

STANCE

When standing in one location for some time, a speaker should place his weight on the forward foot, firmly planted on the floor. His knees should remain flexed; otherwise, fatigue and tension will result. An alert posture, without tension, is an advantage to any speaker or singer.

Experts in sports have found that it pays to seek the most effective way to stand; to hold or swing a golf club, a tennis racket, or ball bat; and to follow other important guidelines. Their seriousness to their profession has caused them to become the experts that they are. They spend endless hours of practice to find out the *why* and the *how* of their pursuit. How much more should we be concerned with the best and most effective delivery of the Word!

SHOULDERS

The speaker should hold his shoulders back and down, but not in a swayback position. Being "spinal" conscious from the top of the head to the base of the body will solve much of his posture problems. Drooped shoulders cause the chest to slump. This suppresses the lungs and deep breathing is hindered. Good posture, however, will help one's appearance as well as his speaking and singing tones.

HEAD AND JAW

The head should be backed up until the base of the skull lines up with the spine, yet leaving the forehead slightly ahead of the chin. This causes the chin to be parallel to the floor. The jaw must be free and floating. Locking the jaw will bring tension to the neck muscles, causing an audible and uneven vibrato or wobble in the sound being produced. On sustained sounds, one

should let his jaw continue to move down and
back through the duration of the tone.

ABDOMEN

The lower abdominal wall should be drawn in
and up. This action will give the speaker firm
support around his waist and hips.

The head, chest, and pelvis should be supported
by the spine in such a way that they align themselves one under the other—head erect, chest
high, pelvis upright. This means that the position
of the head should allow the jaw to be free, not
protruding up and out, nor pulled back into the
throat—thus freeing the organs in the neck. The
high chest implies that the shoulders go back
down, but they should relax and be comfortable.
A certain amount of normal elasticity of the
abdominal muscles will be needed to keep the
pelvis upright; however, there should not be so
much elasticity that deep diaphragmatic breathing
is impossible.

BREATHING

The breathing apparatus consists of the lungs
—with their surrounding rib cage, layered inside

and out with muscles (the diaphragm and abdominal muscles)—and the air passages (the bronchi, the trachea or windpipe, the larynx, and the pharynx). Deep breathing has long been recognized as one of the most wholesome physical habits. The extra oxygen taken in with deep breathing purifies the blood and gives one extra energy. Physicians tell us that asthmatic conditions can often be alleviated by deep breathing exercises.

The diaphragm is the most important single factor in controlling breathing. It is a partition, which separates the chest or thorax from the abdomen; and it consists almost entirely of muscles which come together to a tendon at the center. Though elastic, the diaphragm is very powerful. When at rest, it has the shape of an inverted bowl; but when a person takes a deep breath, it flattens.

The diaphragm's action is up and down, rising and falling as one breathes. As one inhales, or breathes in, his waist enlarges; as he exhales, his abdomen resumes its former shape. Several abdominal muscles—horizontal, vertical, and oblique—assist the diaphragm in pushing out or exhaling the breath.

In conclusion, consider the first question again:

Are you satisfied with your voice? If not, try these helpful hints. They will strengthen a fatigued voice, as well as beautify one's overall tonal quality, if a person is willing to put forth a little effort.